TODAY…

… an Encouraging 7/35 Journey
Hebrews 3:13
Journey 1B

Sandy Picek

Denton, Texas

TODAY ... an Encouraging 7/35 Journey - Life Journey Series - Journey 1

Published by Prodigal Publishing

ISBN- : 978-1-7355383-3-4

Printed in the United States of America

Cover Illustration by: Sandy Picek

What you hold in your hand is what I call "an Encouraging 7/35 journey." It is a different type of journal, or journey, that you can walk through for 35 days and only 7 minutes a day.

Every Journey Date has a true life story, along with encouraging words from God.

There are 35 "journey dates" and at the end of each story, there are 3 questions to think about. You can jot down how something on a given day has touched your heart or impacted you.

We are told, *"But encourage one another daily, as long as it called* <u>*Today*</u>*, so that none of you may be hardened by sin's deceitfulness."-* Hebrews 3:13. My hope is that you will be encouraged by these stories, and feel the touch of Jesus as you read them.

Blessings over you today!

Joyfully in Him,
Sandy

For the many who inspired these stories, but especially to my husband Bill, who loves Jesus and stands by my side here on earth.
And of course Jesus, where would I be without Him!

Journey Date 1_____

Sitting here my mind seems to draw a blank. How unusual that seems to be. Normally my mind is filled with so many things…children, husband, work, friends, God, weather, dinner, laundry, and the list goes on. But today, is just a little different. It's as if God has given my mind a reprieve… "a time out" you might say. As wonderful as that may seem to most of us, there seems to be an underlying feeling of guilt. A guilt that makes me think that I should be "doing something". There are so many things that need to be done, why is there a "blank"? Why is there stillness? Why should I get a "time out"? Why is there quiet, when it appears that the rest of the world around me is in turmoil? Do I really deserve the stillness and time of quiet? Carpe' Diem is where my heart and soul want to be… seizing every moment of life. How can I seize a "blank"? Then all of sudden, a still small voice sounds in my mind… "yes, you deserve to rest, even in these times of turmoil." There it was, the idea that you can seize even the quiet moments in their fullest.

It seems that we hurry and rush and plan and run here and there, and it's difficult to stop and seize the quiet moments. Are you like me, with a sense of feeling guilt if you do stop? Possibly it isn't the stopping of the body that is difficult, but it's the stopping of the mind. Does it race everywhere, wondering, worrying, and wanting, without shutting off? You know, when you lay down at night and it just seems that the brain just won't turn off? I am learning that it really is okay to stop and be "blank" for a moment. Psalm 46:10 says it simply, ***"Be still** and know that I am God…"*

Pretty simple thought… be still, Be Still, BE STILL… just be still and let the world of worries fall away for a moment, and know that God is sitting right there in the stillness with you. It really is okay.

Today, I hope that as your day goes flying by, and life seems to be rushing past, that for just a moment, you will have that "time out". Seize the stillness and bask in the quiet.

****

ASK YOURSELF:

What is God revealing to me today?

_____
_____
_____
_____
_____
_____
_____
_____

How do I see God working in my life today?

_____
_____
_____
_____
_____
_____
_____
_____

What can I do to bring a blessing to someone else?

_____
_____
_____
_____
_____
_____
_____

Journey Date 2_____

Have you ever thought about getting ready for the day, all of the things that you do? I know that I actually "prepare" myself to start the day. I get out of bed, turn on the Keurig, take a shower, go make myself a cup of hot tea, I brush my teeth, dry my hair, get dressed for the day, take my vitamins and then begin to think about what the day holds. If I didn't prepare myself, you probably wouldn't want to be near me. So I do these things each day to bring a freshness for myself in preparing for the new day.

You know it is the same way with our Father and our relationship with Him. He desires to prepare each day for us. He wants us to look for the new adventures of the day. He wants to give us His strength and His Spirit so that we can walk throughout the day in peace and full of joy.

Ephesians 3:16 says, *"I ask the Father in His great glory to give you the power to be strong inwardly through HIS spirit."* I read this and believe that God desires to prepare you for the day and give you His blessings and power through Him. All you have to do is ask and He would love to cover you with these wonderful gifts.

Today, I hope today you know how special you are to Him. You are His and He is yours Be refreshed in peace and joy!

****

ASK YOURSELF:

What is God revealing to me today?

_____
_____
_____
_____
_____
_____
_____
_____

How do I see God working in my life today?

_____
_____
_____
_____
_____
_____
_____
_____

What can I do to bring a blessing to someone else?

_____
_____
_____
_____
_____
_____
_____
_____

Journey Date 3_____

Once again, while driving to work, on a wet and rainy road, it seemed that the curves and bumps were more noticeable. I took notice of the pot holes and the part of the road that was old and beginning to have crevices and cracks. I thought maybe I was on a roller coaster ride, not missing any of the bumpy places and sliding through a couple of slick spots. Then, came a place where the road was brand new. No cracks, no pot holes, no bumps, just flat, straight and easy to cross. The roller coaster ride was coming to a calm and peaceful part of the track. The new road ended and the ride started all over again.

Isn't this what our life is about? Do you ever feel like your life is like that road? Bumpy, slippery, with cracks and crevices and potholes through it? God desires to keep us safe on our road of life. In Psalms 91 we are told, *"Those who go to God Most High for safety will be protected by the Almighty."*

How often do we go to Him for that safety? Or do we try to solve all of our problems and issues in life, our way. By ourselves. He is waiting to smooth out the "rough roads" of life, by protecting, by bringing peace and joy and by loving you.

Today, I encourage you to focus on the part of your life that is like the new road and know that you are in the protection of His mighty hands.

****

ASK YOURSELF:

What is God revealing to me today?

_____
_____
_____
_____
_____
_____
_____
_____

How do I see God working in my life today?

_____
_____
_____
_____
_____
_____
_____
_____
_____

What can I do to bring a blessing to someone else?

_____
_____
_____
_____
_____
_____
_____
_____

Journey Date 4_____

Have you ever wondered about the Spirit of God and where it really is? His spirit is everywhere - can you see it? When was the last time you took a walk through the woods, or drove to the top of a mountain, or walked along a shoreline?

In those places there always seems to be silence, or a breeze blowing, or branches clapping together. Something in those places that seem so much greater than yourself. Awe and wonder strike a "heart chord", and you wish you could touch it. But what about in the tears of your husband or the tears of your wife, in the smile of a little child, in the playfulness of a puppy or a kitten. His Presence is in the rain that falls down and sun that shines. It is in the heart of the person that stands next to you. Just look around you, and you will see His Spirit.

David asks the question in Psalm 139 *"where can I go from your Spirit? Where can I flee from Your Presence?"* We are given the opportunity to see Him in all places, because he does not hide from us. He is everywhere.

Today, look in the eyes of someone you love and then look into your own eyes, and you will see Him there. I see Him daily, I hope you will too.

****

ASK YOURSELF:

What is God revealing to me today?

_____
_____
_____
_____
_____
_____
_____
_____

How do I see God working in my life today?

_____
_____
_____
_____
_____
_____
_____
_____
_____

What can I do to bring a blessing to someone else?

_____
_____
_____
_____
_____
_____
_____
_____

Journey Date 5_____

Imagine yourself in a vast place that is so immense and full of life...
then all of a sudden the lights go out and it is pitch black. You are
there, feeling totally alone, in the darkness, not one glimmer of light
around you. You can't see anything or anyone. You can't hear
anything or anyone. You wonder "how long will I have to stay
here?"

And out of the darkness, in the far away corner there is a tiny
glimmer, almost like a match being lit, and yours eyes become
completely focused on that tiny light. You walk toward it, thinking
if you do, it will lead you out of the darkness. The closer you get the
brighter the light gets. You become more focused, searching for the
"escape door". You just want out of the darkness. You continue to
walk toward the match light. It becomes more like a flashlight, then
like a beacon light... you stay completely focused... when you reach
the light it engulfs you and you stand covered in light and you can
see the door, you can see the pathway to the "outside".

You forget the dark that you were standing in and you go forward.
Psalm 18:16-19 says it this way *"He reached from on high and took
hold of me; He drew me out of deep waters. He rescued me from my
powerful enemy, from my foes, who were too strong for me. They
comfort me in the day of my disaster, but the Lord was my support.
He brought me out into a spacious place; He rescued me because He
delighted in me."*

Today, if you are standing in a dark place whether it is physical,
emotional, mental or financial, HE is holding up the match to guide
you. Focus on the match...you will be bathed in His light.

****

ASK YOURSELF:

What is God revealing to me today?

_____

_____

_____

_____

_____

_____

_____

_____

How do I see God working in my life today?

_____

_____

_____

_____

_____

_____

_____

_____

_____

What can I do to bring a blessing to someone else?

_____

_____

_____

_____

_____

_____

_____

_____

Journey Date 6_____

We have two cats. One of the cats was a real "fraidy" cat. Bill has won her heart over and has brought her out of her shell. How? One simple word … "treats". We found these chewy, soft, chicken flavored cat treats that Chicago Girl loves. Bill and The Girl have a routine every day, where she knows she is going to get some treats. Even better yet, he has trained her to understand the word "treats". All he has to do is say "TREATS" and she comes running. She sits on the floor in front of him, kind of like a dog, waiting for her treats. She knows she won't get any though, until she jumps up on the armrest of the couch and gives Bill a little nudge. But she knows if she does these things, she is going to get a chewy morsel of chicken flavored delights.

Recently though, in her devouring of treats, she left some of the crumbs behind, sitting on the arm rest. In the meantime, Bill got himself an evening snack of cookies and milk, and set the cookies on the armrest while he was getting comfortable. Not knowing that The Girl had left some of her tasty morsels behind. He picked up his cookies and began to eat them. He noticed that there were some "crumbs" left on the armrest, and picked them up and threw them in his mouth. No sense in wasting good cookie crumbs. Quickly he realized that in the midst of the cookie crumbs was a leftover cat treat. Ugh! How awful was that! The cat treat actually looked like a small morsel of the cookie. But, oh, it did NOT taste like a yummy cookie at all.

This was a perfect example though of what we fall prey to. How many times do we see something that we think we must have and we buy it, only to feel guilty later. Or possibly that we are tempted to do something that we know will be harmful in the long run, but our mind convinces us that "it" won't be that bad if we only do "it" once. Or, we long to be in a relationship with someone so desperately that we settle for a companion who brings more pain than love. The bottom line on all of these things is deception. Just like the little cat treat, it was hiding itself amongst the yummy cookie crumbs. Bill couldn't even tell the difference, but as soon as he tasted it, he knew it was bad.

It is so easy to be deceived by money, power and relationships. Yet, we have a wonderful Savior who will protect us from the deception when we ask Him to. Several times Christ tells us, "do not be deceived" … "follow me and you will receive your reward in Heaven." Maybe you are on a road that just doesn't feel right, and you wonder why. Maybe you are considering a turn in your life that doesn't fit what you know is true. Ask our Lord to show you the truth, and to make the path clear and without deception.

Today, truth awaits each and every one of us. It's God's promise to us. His truth will set us free, and free indeed we will be.

****

ASK YOURSELF:

What is God revealing to me today?

_____

_____

_____

_____

_____

How do I see God working in my life today?

_____

_____

_____

_____

_____

What can I do to bring a blessing to someone else?

_____

_____

_____

_____

_____

Journey Date 7_____

When was the last time that you went to an art gallery? My children are very creative and have a great ability to capture their love of life in their talents of drawing, painting and photography, and have had several pieces of their work entered into art contests and made it to the gallery.

Every time I go and look at the many different aspects of art I am fascinated at how each piece is so individual. Each person that created their work, took time, effort and exactness to make their masterpiece to look exactly like it looks. Every brush stroke is important, until the final one is placed, and the artist signs their name to the work. Every pencil line on the drawing, every piece of paper placed on the mache', and the countless numbers of photographs until the perfect one is taken. Every piece has a beginning and an end, and along the way there are touch ups and re-dos and then all of sudden, there it is... the finished product!
Perfection at the end!

Do you know that you are the same way? Every day is a new stroke of the brush by God. He is preparing you for the perfection that HE sees in you. Philippians 1:6 tells us, *"He who began a good work in you, will see it to completion until the day of Jesus Christ."* You see, God started his good work with you the day you were being formed in your mother's womb, and each day He places one more pencil line, one more brush stroke, one more polishing of the silver until your day of completion, which will be when we are facing Christ. We are all in the place of being formed for the perfection of Him. That's it. Nothing more, nothing less, BUT, we are being placed here on earth by Him to share about HIS perfection, not ours.

Today you may not be perfect, but you are being painted on. What a beautiful picture God is painting as HE paints you! He has signed His name on you because YOU are His masterpiece!

****

ASK YOURSELF:

What is God revealing to me today?

_____
_____
_____
_____
_____
_____
_____
_____

How do I see God working in my life today?

_____
_____
_____
_____
_____
_____
_____
_____
_____

What can I do to bring a blessing to someone else?

_____
_____
_____
_____
_____
_____
_____

Journey Date 8_____

Have you ever woken up with that "starving" hungry feeling? You know, the one where your stomach is growling so loud that you think it will wake everyone up in the house. That feeling of, "if I don't get something to eat or drink quickly, I may just pass out." Have you ever had that feeling? You are so hungry you just HAVE to have something to fill that emptiness in your belly or there may be some major consequences to the pantry?

We are the same way with our emotions and our heart. There are times we have that empty hungry feeling in our soul and we are longing for something to fill it. Something that will give us complete satisfaction. Longing for a relationship that will never run dry, but is always fulfilling. Have you ever had that feeling? Are you longing for the empty space in your heart to be filled? That something is Jesus.

John 6:35 says, *"I am the bread of life. He who comes to ME will never go hungry and he who believes in ME will never be thirsty. "*

Today are you feeling hungry or thirsty, or do you have that "empty place" inside of you? Call out the name above all names... and He will satisfy you to never feel that emptiness again.

****

ASK YOURSELF:

What is God revealing to me today?

_____

_____

_____

_____

_____

_____

_____

_____

How do I see God working in my life today?

_____

_____

_____

_____

_____

_____

_____

_____

_____

What can I do to bring a blessing to someone else?

_____

_____

_____

_____

_____

_____

_____

_____

Journey Date 9_____

Have you ever been on a train ride? Our family took a train ride several years ago through the Colorado mountains. There were parts of the ride that the scenery was so breath taking, that you knew God was standing beside you. Then there were the tunnels. As we would approach the tunnel, I would wonder how long was the tunnel, how long would it be dark, when would we reach the other side? I always knew that there would be light at the end of the tunnel, I just didn't know when I would see it. It seemed like such an uneasy feeling to be in the unending beauty of the Colorado mountains, but couldn't see it.

 Our lives are the same way. You may be approaching a tunnel or maybe you have been in the tunnel for a while and you are just waiting to see the breaking light and the beauty of God. Or, you may be standing on the other side of the tunnel, breathing in the freshness of God... wherever you are, I want to remind you of what God tells us in Isaiah. Read the words below and put your name in the blank and know that He will never leave you or forsake you.

"Fear not _____, I have redeemed you; I the Lord have called you by your name; you are Mine. When you pass through the waters, I will be with you; and through the rivers, they shall not overflow you. When you walk through the fire, you will not be burned and the flame will not scorch you. _____,
you are Mine!" - Isaiah 43: 1 & 2

Today, remember that our Savior is right beside you in the darkness and will be with you through the "tunnel" of life.

****

ASK YOURSELF:

What is God revealing to me today?

_____
_____
_____
_____
_____
_____
_____
_____

How do I see God working in my life today?

_____
_____
_____
_____
_____
_____
_____
_____

What can I do to bring a blessing to someone else?

_____
_____
_____
_____
_____
_____
_____
_____

Journey Date 10_____

My dog, Charlie, is getting old. He is coming up on 12 years now. You know that proverbial statement, "Do you want to go outside" always gets a dog up and running. Well, lately it doesn't even move him off of the couch (yes, he does get on our couch). We thought maybe was losing interest in going outside as often, and just enjoyed resting on the couch or laying on the floor, or just relaxing as an older dog will do. But we realized that he had become hard of hearing. If we get really close to him and speak very loud, he perks up out of his restful place and trots over to the door. I have watched him over time and see how much he ignores (because he can't hear) all of the outside noises. Nothing bothers him anymore. He just rests.

I thought about this and realized we can do the same thing. Not that we want to be hard of hearing, but that we can rest in our Lord. When we stop the "outside noises" (possibly the voice of our greatest enemy) and listen to the voice of our Lord we can rest in our circumstances and know that HE will take care of us. *Psalm 91:1 and Matthew 11:28 tell us, "He who dwells in the shelter of the Most High will REST in the Shadow of the Almighty"* and Jesus says, *"Come to ME all who are weary and burdened and I will give you REST."*

My dear friends and family, no matter what you are going through, I pray that you will close your ears for just a moment to the noise that may be confusing or painful and REST in the calming words of our Lord.

Today, rest on the couch, lay on the floor, or just sit at your desk and let HIM bathe you in His shelter.

****

ASK YOURSELF:

What is God revealing to me today?

_____
_____
_____
_____
_____
_____
_____
_____

How do I see God working in my life today?

_____
_____
_____
_____
_____
_____
_____
_____

What can I do to bring a blessing to someone else?

_____
_____
_____
_____
_____
_____
_____
_____

Journey Date 11_____

Today it seems that the word "life" means "to hurry". How many times in a day do you hurry to get all of your chores done? How many times do you tell your children or your co-workers that we need to "hurry up and get this done because we have so many other things to do". How many meetings, soccer games, rehearsals, and deadlines do we all have on our platter each day?

Some days the platter seems like it is so full that we just want to stop and yell "NO MORE!" Even when we think we are accomplishing the things that need to be done, and start peeling the pieces off of the platter, more gets added and the platter seems to never be empty. Then the toppings on the platter become piled with stress, then a little anxiety is poured on, and then worry and depression may become the final topping.

David tells us in the Psalms that we need to be still and know that God is our refuge and strength. *"God is our refuge and strength, an ever-present help in trouble. Therefore we will not fear..." Psalms 46:1.* God tells us in Psalm 46:10 - *"Be STILL and know that I AM GOD!"*

Today as your "life" continues to bring new challenges, I encourage that to take the time to stop and be still. Turn off the TV, turn off the Smartphone or computer, and if you can, go into your closet and rest in Him. Be still and know that HE is God. HE is your refuge.

****

ASK YOURSELF:

What is God revealing to me today?

_____

_____

_____

_____

_____

_____

_____

_____

How do I see God working in my life today?

_____

_____

_____

_____

_____

_____

_____

_____

_____

What can I do to bring a blessing to someone else?

_____

_____

_____

_____

_____

_____

_____

_____

Journey Date 12_____

Every day I drive to and from work I pass by a landfill. I have
noticed in the hot afternoons that there is usually a flock of buzzards
flying in the sky over this lovely piece of land. As we all know,
buzzards or vultures as you may call them, look for the dying
"specimen". They perch for hours watching and waiting for their
prey to take its last breath, and then they go in for the devouring. As
I have taken notice of these creatures I find that they are very
persistent. They fly and they watch, and they fly and they watch,
never taking their eyes off of their victim. When their prey finally
gives in to death, they go in and destroy what is left of the dying
animal and the buzzards have their feast. Have you ever thought if
only the animal would run for safety or go and hide somewhere the
buzzards could not get to it?

You may feel like you are in a "landfill" and it seems that death is all
around you, and the "buzzards" are flying over your head waiting for
you to fall. I tell you today, that Jesus says *"I AM the bread of life.
He who comes to Me will never be hungry and he who believes in
Me will never be thirsty."* He tells us, *"The thief comes only to steal
and kill and destroy; but I have come that you may have life and
have it to the fullest."* (John 6:35 and John 10:10)

If you are feeling like the specimen and the buzzards are watching
remember that God is watching you too. He is wanting you to run to
Him and hide in Him so that He may give you life and take care of
you. He does not want your enemy to devour you, but He wants to
give you a fresh drink.

Today, I pray that you will feel His comfort all around you, and
believe that He is covering you with arms of peace.

****

ASK YOURSELF:

What is God revealing to me today?

_____
_____
_____
_____
_____
_____
_____
_____

How do I see God working in my life today?

_____
_____
_____
_____
_____
_____
_____
_____
_____

What can I do to bring a blessing to someone else?

_____
_____
_____
_____
_____
_____
_____
_____

Journey Date 13_____

My husband and I owned three vehicles. One of them was born in 1995 and two were born in 1996. Needless to say they are all having some "issues" and in need of "road repair". My father graciously let us borrow his 1995 Cadillac Sedan Deville, while he had been on vacation. He told us that the car needed an oil change, and if we wouldn't mind, could we get it done. So my husband took the car to our usual place. He drove up and a new fellow popped the hood and just stood there in amazement. He came in and looked at my husband and just said "WOW man - I don't think I've ever seen a car so clean". Now I know my father, he takes great care of his vehicles. He "cleans" the engine with that "engine degreaser cleaner stuff". And he changes the oil regularly and rotates the tires and does all the things that it takes to keep the car running in good shape. I can remember him always telling me that however you care for your vehicle, is how it will return its use.

As goofy as it sounds, we are like my dad's Cadillac. If we ask our Father in Heaven to keep us clean and "change our oil" and "rotate our tires" He will give us a "clean heart". I love what Psalm 51 says: *"Create in me a clean heart, O God and renew a steadfast spirit within me. Do not cast me from Your Presence or take Your Holy Spirit from me. Restore to me the joy of Your salvation and grant me a willing spirit to sustain me."* Psalm 51: 10-12

"Create In Me A Clean Heart" is one of my favorite songs to sing. I hope that you will sing these words to your Father and let Him give you and oil change today.

Today, let Him clean and renew you with His Holy Spirit and restore your joy.

****

ASK YOURSELF:

What is God revealing to me today?

_____
_____
_____
_____
_____
_____
_____
_____

How do I see God working in my life today?

_____
_____
_____
_____
_____
_____
_____
_____

What can I do to bring a blessing to someone else?

_____
_____
_____
_____
_____
_____
_____
_____

Journey Date 14_____

I have a friend who shared a great story with me, and I would like to pass on to you. She has a little boy, who just turned 6. As a younger boy his parents had given him a children's Bible. You know, the ones with the short abbreviated stories and very colorful pictures. It was a beginning place for him to learn to know who God and Jesus were. My friend tells me that he loved his Bible and carried it proudly. As he has reached this "old age" of 6, the little boy was given a "Big" Bible. She said his eyes got huge and was so excited to get a "big person's" Bible. He apparently took the Bible to his room and glanced through the new crisp pages and began reading at Genesis 1. Then he came out to talk to his mom and said with such innocence "mommy, do I have to read this whole thing in one night?"

What an amazing desire to learn more and search for God at such a young age.

If we could only be like this little boy. Hungering and thirsting to want to know the "whole" story of Lord. Jesus tells us to come him as little children, just trusting and loving and desiring. *"Let the little children come to Me, and do not hinder them, for the Kingdom of God belongs to such as these. I tell you the truth, anyone who will not receive the Kingdom of God like a little child will never enter it."* - Matthew 19:14, Mark 10:14, Luke 18:16.

Today let your hunger and thirst be as my friends' little boy, carrying God's word proudly with you, longing to know the whole story of a Savior who died, so we could live.

****

ASK YOURSELF:

What is God revealing to me today?

_____

_____

_____

_____

_____

_____

_____

_____

How do I see God working in my life today?

_____

_____

_____

_____

_____

_____

_____

_____

_____

What can I do to bring a blessing to someone else?

_____

_____

_____

_____

_____

_____

_____

_____

Journey Date 15_____

Some time ago, my family added a new addition to it. No I am not a grandmother, NOR have I had more children... but we do have a gray and white tiger stripped kitten. My daughter Katy and I came up with the name "Chicago Girl" (that is another story in itself). If you have ever had a kitten or a puppy you will understand the passion for playfulness that is born within them. Then on the other hand, they are still trying to figure out how to stay "protected" from the "big bad uglies" out there (like our German Sheperd Charlie) and where to go for rest and feel safe. Chicago Girl has found her resting place... it is in my daughter Katy. She will run for Katy's room when she feels afraid and Katy will pick her up and pet her and hold her close and talk to her calmly. Then Chicago girl will curl up around Katy's neck or on Katy's stomach and just lay and rest and fall sound asleep. All of the cares in the world could be crashing down around her, but Chicago Girl knows that she is safe in Katy's presence.

We are like Chicago Girl. Life hands us many circumstances that seem to keep us running. Some of them are good circumstance, and many of them are difficult. Your life may be full of the "big bad uglies", it may be so full that you feel there is no place to run and feel protected and at rest.

Jesus is your resting place. He is the one you can run to, and hide in His presence. He will let you curl up next to Him and He will hold you close and bring you comfort. Jesus tells us in Matthew, *"Come to ME, all you who are weary and heavy burdened, and I will give you rest. Take MY yoke upon you and learn from Me, for I am gentle and humble in heart, and you will find rest for your souls. For My yoke is easy and my burden is light"*.: - Matthew 11:28-29

Today run to Him and leap in His arms and rest. We all need to rest. My prayer for you is that you will know His presence is there with you, bringing you rest and peaceful moments.

****

ASK YOURSELF:

What is God revealing to me today?

_____

_____

_____

_____

_____

_____

_____

_____

How do I see God working in my life today?

_____

_____

_____

_____

_____

_____

_____

_____

What can I do to bring a blessing to someone else?

_____

_____

_____

_____

_____

_____

_____

_____

Journey Date 16_____

Last night I took our kitten, Chicago Girl, to get her first set of shots. As I was putting her in the cat carrier, she thought it was fun... at first. Then she realized I was locking the door and carrying her outside. She scrambled around in the carrier for a minute or so and then we took off in the truck. I could tell by her meowing and pacing back and forth in the carrier that she wasn't quite sure of what was going on. Each time she meowed, I would talk to her. I would speak in a soft voice and tell her "it's okay, we will be there soon". I would call out her name "Chicago Girl - sweet kitty - it's okay, I am here for you." She knew my voice which seemed to give her comfort for just the moments she could hear it, but then she would cry again.

Our drive was about 10 minutes to the vet, but to her, it must have seemed like hours. When we arrived at our destination, I took her in the carrier and gave her to the veterinarian. She got her shots and we went back to the truck. I opened the cage and she calmly walked out and crawled in my lap. She knew she had to trust me to get her back home safely. I continued to talk to her and hold her close and then opened the door of the carrier. Willingly she went back inside and laid down. It was as if she knew she had to trust me and not her own instincts.

Proverbs 3:5-6 tells us to do same thing with our lives and God. *"Trust in the Lord with ALL your heart and lean not on your own understanding, in ALL your ways acknowledge Him and He shall direct your paths."* God knows what place you are in. He knows the "cat carrier" of your life and hears you calling out to Him. He knows the pains, the hurts, the heartaches, the trials. He knows the joy, the laughter and the tears that you cry.

Today know His Presence is in your path, and even for a moment, tell Him you trust Him with your life and your circumstances and HE will take care of you.

****

ASK YOURSELF:

What is God revealing to me today?

_____
_____
_____
_____
_____
_____
_____
_____

How do I see God working in my life today?

_____
_____
_____
_____
_____
_____
_____
_____
_____

What can I do to bring a blessing to someone else?

_____
_____
_____
_____
_____
_____
_____
_____

Journey Date 17_____

Have you ever left your car running for a long period of time, parked in one spot? My son parked our GEO Tracker at school one rainy day and he proceeded to take the key out of the ignition and head for class.   At 2:04 PM he takes his afternoon trip back to the car, ready to unlock the door, and he noticed that his car keys were missing. As the rain kept coming down, he realized the car was running. His keychain snaps apart, and he thought he taken the entire set, but the car key was still in the ignition and the car was never turned off. It sat in one place, for almost six hours, running idly, but not moving. Now fortunately it was still sitting in the same place. (I call that a miracle, even if it is a 1995 GEO Tracker). I have thought about this incident; gas being pumped into the engine, the engine NEVER being turned off, and yet the car didn't go anywhere. Obviously it didn't go anywhere because there wasn't a driver. No one to steer the wheel or to shift the gears. No one to give the car direction.

There are times that I feel like I am that car in my realationship with God. My engine continues to run, sometimes a million miles an hour, but I don't get anywhere. I don't let God put me in gear or turn the steering wheel. I try to do it myself or I just park myself in my self-pity or in my difficult circumstances and I use up all of the fuel. One of God's greatest promises is found in Jeremiah 29. Let me write it out here:

"For I know the plans I have for you", <u>DECLARES the Lord</u>, *"plans to prosper you and not to harm you, plans to give you hope and a future. Then you will call upon ME and come and pray to Me, and I WILL listen to you."* - Jeremiah 29: 11 & 12

You see God has such great plans for you, and for me, if we will just let Him drive our life. It isn't just that he "says" He has a plan for us... He DECLARES IT! Isn't that exciting?! I hope today that He will steer your "vehicle" and you will know that He is driving you in the right direction.

Today, may the greatest driver of all, be your guide.

****

ASK YOURSELF:

What is God revealing to me today?

_____
_____
_____
_____
_____
_____
_____
_____

How do I see God working in my life today?

_____
_____
_____
_____
_____
_____
_____
_____
_____

What can I do to bring a blessing to someone else?

_____
_____
_____
_____
_____
_____
_____
_____

Journey Date 18_____

There is so much on my mind today that I just can't seem to focus on one thing. There are many people in my life who are dealing with different heartaches, pains and sufferings. Several friends of mine are dealing with cancer, brain cancer, lung cancer and breast cancer. I have a friend who is struggling in their marriage. Another friend longs for communication with their children. Yet another friend desires to have a baby. My sister had some negative test results on her pap smear, twice, as well as undergoing long treatment of a bladder disease. Another friend's 7 year old daughter is in the process of having major dental surgery and having her teeth extracted. Many others are recovering from the loss of a dear loved one and others are suffering from the loss of their financial income. Another of my friends wakes up every day wondering what else can happen to their physical health, and others who just want to wake up and breathe a breath of fresh air to get them through their depression.

As I sat and prayed and thought about the many people whom I love, who God has put in my path, (you), I thought there is no way that I can help or do anything to give them comfort or peace. Clearly He showed me, "you are right, you can't, but "I - GOD" can!" Words from our Savior tell us ....

"Peace I leave with you, MY peace I give to you, not as the world gives do I give to you. Let not your heart be troubled, neither let it be afraid." - John 14:27

Today, you may recognize yourself in one of these places, or several of these places. If you are reading these words, I have prayed for you. I promise you that Jesus will give you the peace that you long for. As you read these words I hope that you feel His presence and know HIS peace is blanketing you now.

****

ASK YOURSELF:

What is God revealing to me today?

_____
_____
_____
_____
_____
_____
_____
_____

How do I see God working in my life today?

_____
_____
_____
_____
_____
_____
_____
_____
_____

What can I do to bring a blessing to someone else?

_____
_____
_____
_____
_____
_____
_____
_____

Journey Date 19_____

I remember growing up and hearing the saying, "Absence makes the heart grow fonder." I wasn't too sure of what that meant until I got older. You know what that message really means, right?... "Leave now honey, because you are driving me crazy, and I need some time alone - but don't be gone too long, because I will miss you soon." In years past my husband traveled quite a bit. He would be gone two or three weeks at a time and then return for a weekend and then depart again. As a family, we began to get use to his schedule and "know" that he would return. But Charlie, our German Shepherd, wasn't always so sure of that. No matter if Bill was gone one day or one month, Charlie would ALWAYS great him with a hug and a smile that only a dog could give (literally the dog would get up on the bed and put his paws on Bills' shoulders and lay his head on on Bills' chest).

I have thought about this saying lately and realized it is not a very good statement when you want a relationship to grow. I think time apart helps me to understand how much I desire to have a "daily" relationship with my husband, not just the weekends. Charlie doesn't know any different, he just knows that he is to "love" on Bill every time Bill walks through the door.

We should be like Charlie with our relationship with God. God so desires for us to have that "daily' relationship with Him. He doesn't want to wait for weekends when "we" walk through "His" doors. He wants us to develop that relationship every single day and not wait to be absent from Him to have a closer relationship. Jesus is asked what the greatest commandment is. His response is found in Mark 12:30 – *"Love the Lord your God, with all of your heart, with all of your soul and with all of your mind, and all of your strength."*

Today, no matter where you are with God, tell Him how much you love Him and let Him walk into the door of your heart.

****

ASK YOURSELF:

What is God revealing to me today?

_____
_____
_____
_____
_____
_____
_____
_____

How do I see God working in my life today?

_____
_____
_____
_____
_____
_____
_____
_____
_____

What can I do to bring a blessing to someone else?

_____
_____
_____
_____
_____
_____
_____
_____

Journey Date 20_____

Yesterday I was at the gym working out. I always take my own
music so that I can listen to I want to. There I was riding on the
bike, listening to the album that I chose, and it seemed that my music
was getting softer, or the music in the gym was getting louder. I
turned up my music to "drown out" the music at the gym. Then
there were people who got on other machines that were near me.
One was making a really loud noise as they walked on the treadmill.
The other person was talking to someone next to them and because
the music was so loud in the gym, they were talking loud. So, I
turned up MY music again, just a little bit louder to try and "drown
out" more noise. I kept peddling, trying to focus on the music that
was now seemingly blaring in my ears… then some fellows decided
to play basketball on the courts, so now I could hear the thumping of
the basketball and the whopping and yelling on the courts. I finally
decided to just give in and turn the music up as loud as it could go –
which may have caused some deafness, but I wanted to focus on MY
music and not everything else around me.

Our lives are much like this. So many things creep into our lives
that take over the focus of our lives. Surely you know what I mean.
First off, our jobs – how much attention does it get? Then our
family, then our church, then our friends, then our pets, then comes
illnesses along the way, or disaster's, or death, or even the fun events
in our life. We must always remember that God is our first focus in
ALL of these things.

God tells us in Isaiah 55: 3 - *"Listen carefully to ME, and eat what is
good. And let your soul delight itself in abundance. Incline your
ear, and come to ME. Hear, and your soul shall live. And I WILL
make an everlasting covenant with you."*

Isn't that awesome! All we have to do is listen with our ears and
come near to God and He has promised us an everlasting covenant
with Him. I don't know what "things" you are trying to "drown
out", so stop for just a moment, even if it is right now, and spend 30
seconds just in silence, listening to God. It may be hard for you to
stop… but I urge you to take a moment for yourself and try it.

Today may God bless you and may you see that He makes Himself real in a special way.

****

ASK YOURSELF:

What is God revealing to me today?

_____
_____
_____
_____
_____
_____
_____

How do I see God working in my life today?

_____
_____
_____
_____
_____
_____
_____
_____

What can I do to bring a blessing to someone else?

_____
_____
_____
_____
_____
_____
_____

Journey Date 21_____

One Sunday morning I decided to attend the "early, early" service at church. I left the house at 8:00 am and drove about 1 mile and it seemed as though I was driving into a cloud. As I kept driving, I realized I really was driving in a cloud. It was the strangest feeling. The sky was dull yellow and I could sense the sun was really trying to creep through the clouds, but the further I drove, the denser the cloud became. In order to get to my church I had to drive down two lane, bumpy, curvy country roads. Here it was – the sky was "suppose" to be light, but it wasn't, the roads are usually clear, but they weren't, using headlights on the car is not usually necessary, but it was. The best word's that comes to my mind about what was going on around me is "eerie uneasiness". I don't even know if those words go together, but that is how I felt while driving. I couldn't see five feet in front of me. I could barely see the yellow stripes in the road. Yet I knew that the sun was shining somewhere above me, but I couldn't see that either.

Then it dawned on me (or actually I think it was probably the Holy Spirit talking to me) – this is like the relationship between me and Jesus. It's like me to get in my car and "believe" that "I" am in the driver's seat, going where "I" want to go and Jesus is going "with" me, but "I" am still driving and WHAM – there it is, the cloud that has been waiting to drop on "my" life. I start asking myself "where are you Lord? – I can't see where I am going – have you abandoned me? My life is bumpy, and curves are being tossed in front of me and everything seems so hazy… (and I shout out) **WHERE ARE YOU LORD?"**

The great news is that as I continued to drive to church, the clouds began to rise a little. The closer I got to church, the clouds got lighter and lighter. Finally, the church was only half a mile away and the cloud was totally gone. I could see again! Hallelujah! The fog was lifted, the streets were clear, I could see the yellow dividing lines in the road.

Isn't that like Jesus – HE never really left me, I was doing the "driving" through the fog, and the clouds and the choices that I made. But, HE wanted to be the one driving all along, and as I drew nearer to Him, everything became so clear. God's promise in Deuteronomy 31:8 is that *"He will never leave us or forsake us"*.... NEVER!

Today, if you are driving down that road of despair, loneliness, fear, doubt, shame, unworthiness, ugliness, un-forgiveness, selfishness, or any other road, remember that Jesus is just a glimpse behind the clouds. All you have to do is leave the driving up to Him.

****

ASK YOURSELF:

What is God revealing to me today?

_____
_____
_____
_____
_____

How do I see God working in my life today?

_____
_____
_____
_____
_____

What can I do to bring a blessing to someone else?

_____
_____
_____
_____
_____
_____
_____

Sometime ago my husband I decided to "re-do" the master bedroom closet. Myhusband wanted to give the closet a make-over or in other words, restore it back to being a closet and not a "junk pile" or "collector's bin". Naturally, to do that EVERYTHING has to come out of the closet. I hate to admit this, I always say that my husband is the pack rat, but, true confession is, this time it was all me. I had clothes two sizes too small, two sizes too big (that's always a good thing), boxes of papers, the original "wedding box" (this is the box of memories from when Bill and I got hitched), shoes too small, shoes too big, shoes I haven't worn in three years…. The list could go on and on.

We finally got it all out. Bill ripped out the old shelves and put up beautiful new, white, double decked shelves. The closet seemed so much bigger and roomy. Then came the time to put everything back in the closet. You can probably guess where I am going with this… not EVERYTHING was put back in the closet. I think I had two bags of trash and old clothes that I was NOT putting back in. The trash went right where it belonged and the clothes went to a recycle container. I had so much space now that the clothes neatly hung on the racks, and the shoes are up on the shelf. As crazy as this may sound, I am really proud of my closet. My husband did an awesome job in "restoring" the old junked up closet to a beautiful, pleasant closet to walk in to. I hope to keep it this way.

It dawned on me that I am the same way with God. I store up in my mind, my heart, my body and my spirit, EVERYTHING that I have done wrong or bad or hurtful, and the place in my heart for God becomes a "collector's bin" of trash and unneeded things. I stock pile so much stuff that it is difficult for me to hear God. Sometimes I cry out to God, "aren't you listening to me?" – when in reality I should be saying - "why can't I hear you God?" After seeing the restoration of my closet, I realized that He isn't "stuffing the heart full of junk" – I am.

Psalm 51:12 says, *"Restore to me the joy of your salvation and grant me a willing spirit to sustain me."* This is what I want from God, to restore to me the joy of HIS salvation and to give me a willing spirit to keep me that way. It is difficult not to shove "junk" into the closet of our heart, but with God's power, mercy and grace He will help to restore us.

Today is your "closet" cluttered? Let God will restore HIS joy to you, and remove the "junk" from your heart.

****

ASK YOURSELF:

What is God revealing to me today?

_____

_____

_____

_____

_____

_____

How do I see God working in my life today?

_____

_____

_____

_____

_____

_____

What can I do to bring a blessing to someone else?

_____

_____

_____

_____

_____

_____

_____

Journey Date 23_____

Have you ever made a new Resolution to change something? I try not to, because it seems that I always break them. You know, that proverbial one "I AM going to loose weight this year!" (That is the number one resolution made each year.) Then of course when you fail at keeping your resolution, you feel bad. Emotions and inside thoughts of self-condemnation and feeling like a failure show up.

Let me encourage you today to know that God never fails at His resolutions. He always comes through, even when you feel like your fire is about to go out or you are at a breaking point. He promises us in Isaiah 43:2 - *"A bruised reed He will not break and a smoldering wick He will not put out, but He will bring justice and truth."*

When you feel like your flame is dying or you can no longer keep the "resolution", God is there to hold you up and keep your fire stoked.

Maybe you are okay, but the person next to you looks like the broken reed... I encourage you to help them stand and give them a fresh drink today by your smile and your words.

Today, may the Lord restore the fire, take away the condemnation and pour His blessings upon you.

****

ASK YOURSELF:

What is God revealing to me today?

_____

_____

_____

_____

_____

_____

_____

_____

How do I see God working in my life today?

_____

_____

_____

_____

_____

_____

_____

_____

_____

What can I do to bring a blessing to someone else?

_____

_____

_____

_____

_____

_____

_____

_____

Journey Date 24_____

Many of you have heard me talk about my German Shepherd, Charlie, and the many things that I learned from him. Well Charlie is no longer with us. For several months he began having problems walking, and then more problems with his bladder. We took him to the vet to have him checked out, only to find that he had over 20 bladder stones and acute arthritis in his back, both back hips and all of his legs. After asking the opinion of the vet of how to treat Charlie, and having Charlie in "doggie diapers" for three months and watching him cry when he went up and down the stairs, we finally decided that it was time to let him go. Charlie was 15 years old. But it was my loving husband who decided to give Charlie his "last supper", or breakfast as it may be. My husband got up and made a pan of brownies, bacon and eggs, biscuits, gravy and sausage. We sat out on the patio and had breakfast with Charlie. We gave him one of our good plates, filled it with all of the goodies and watched him enjoy every bite. He didn't know what was about to happen, but he so enjoyed the moment of being with us, outside where he loved to be, eating everything that he knew was too good to be true… especially the chocolate brownies!

Charlie has been gone now for some time. I don't know why this image has been so clear in mind lately, except that as I write it, I am reminded that Charlie lived every moment for the moment. He didn't think about "what is going to happen to me", he just loved the moment. So many times I miss the moment, because I get so caught up in the "what if's", and "what now's". I could learn a lesson from my precious Charlie… live today for today.

In *Matthew 6: 25 Jesus tells us, "do not worry about your life, what you will eat or drink, or about your body and what you will wear. Is not life more important than food, and the body more important than the clothes you wear?"*

Today as your day goes by, look for the moments of joy right before your eyes. Take a few moments and pass on your worries to God and let Him take care of you and enjoy the chocolate brownies of life.

****

ASK YOURSELF:

What is God revealing to me today?

_____
_____
_____
_____
_____
_____
_____
_____

How do I see God working in my life today?

_____
_____
_____
_____
_____
_____
_____
_____

What can I do to bring a blessing to someone else?

_____
_____
_____
_____
_____
_____
_____
_____

Journey Date 25_____

A few years ago my step-mother gave me a book called, "90 Minutes in Heaven". She told me that once I started reading it, that I wouldn't want to stop until I got to the end. She was correct. I have heard so many stories about different people who have "died and gone to Heaven", that I wondered how this book would be any different. It was. While reading the book I thought about those loved ones that have preceded me. My mom, my father-in-law, my grandfather and grandmother, my dear friends' daughter, my two friends mother's, and so many more. After reading this book, I realized that there are no words that can bring comfort to the hurting here on earth, but oh my friend, the comfort that is in Heaven… how marvelous! No more pain. No more aches. No more sorrow. No more worry. No more debt. It truly must be a place that we cannot comprehend here on Earth, unless God chooses to let us have that "90 Minutes in Heaven", but the only way to get there is through the saving grace of Jesus.

The reason I am writing this is to ask you that one question… have you let Jesus take residence in your heart? He came and suffered here on earth, so that we would have a place of beauty to live in for eternity. I love what Jesus tells us in the book of John 10:27-30. *"My sheep listen to my voice; I know them, and they follow Me.* ***I give them eternal life and they shall never perish;*** *no one can snatch them out of My hand. My Father, who has given them to Me, is greater than all; no one can snatch them out of my Father's hand. I and the father are one."* Oh my friend, time is SO short

Today my prayer is that, if you have never asked Jesus to reside in your heart, that you would read these words again, and seek Him…He is waiting for you. If you do know Jesus as your personal Savior, then maybe share this message with a friend

****

ASK YOURSELF:

What is God revealing to me today?

_____

_____

_____

_____

_____

_____

_____

_____

How do I see God working in my life today?

_____

_____

_____

_____

_____

_____

_____

_____

What can I do to bring a blessing to someone else?

_____

_____

_____

_____

_____

_____

_____

_____

Journey Day 26 _____

Have you ever been in a downpour of rain? I am not sure if where you live, you have these type of rains, but up here in the Denton Country, it can pour down so hard that even my big, not afraid of anything, Samson kitty, will hide. The rains come so quickly that many of the roads flood as fast as the rain falls down. One time I decided to go out after the rains had stopped, and noticed many of the "gullies" and small creeks had risen so high that there was debris and trash all over the place. Items like old tires, metal pieces, partial fences, logs, I even saw a shoe laying on the banks of a creek. You could see how high the floods had gone with the leftover "spillage" of the water. I thought how ugly and nasty everything looked after the water had subsided.

Then it dawned on me, these "gullies" were like my mouth. No, I don't mean I have debris such as tires and shoes in my mouth, but I do have "spillage" that comes out of my mouth. Not that I want to admit that, but I do. One time I said something that I wish I had kept in my mouth, but it was too late. The flood of the words came out, and what was left behind was not pretty.

Then I found it… Jesus talking… Matthew 12:34-37 (Paraphrased) *"For out of the overflow of the heart the mouth speaks. The good man brings good things out of the good stored up in him, and the evil man brings evil things out of the evil stored up in him…But I, Jesus, tell you that men will have to give account on the day of judgement for every word they speak."* Oh Lord, forgive me… oh my friends and family, forgive me for anytime that I may have spoken words of unkindness.

Today I pray that you receive the good things that are stored up for you, and the "spillage" does not fall close to you.

****

ASK YOURSELF:

What is God revealing to me today?

_____
_____
_____
_____
_____
_____
_____
_____

How do I see God working in my life today?

_____
_____
_____
_____
_____
_____
_____
_____

What can I do to bring a blessing to someone else?

_____
_____
_____
_____
_____
_____
_____
_____

Journey Day 27 _____

Not too long ago, I went into a store and noticed that incense was burning. It has been quite some time since I burned incense, but I remember the times when I did. It was to "escape" the place that I was in and I wanted to "relax" and know that with the gentle scent I would feel like all of my troubles and fears would disappear for a while. As I stood there, I could see the small pillar of smoke making its way out of the dome like incense holder. It was a lavender scent, soft and calming, yet strong enough to make the entire place smell of this aroma.

I began to think of the wise men who brought incense to Jesus. Now what would a baby do with incense? I believe it was for Mary and Joseph to burn, to receive that calmness that the Lord had to offer them. I imagine as they burned it they gave their praises for the Savior that was born and to God Almighty who sent this little child. Though they were in an "unusual" and "difficult" circumstance, I can imagine God speaking to them, giving them a certain comfort that their prayers and concerns were being heard. Their prayers were filling the room and the Heavens above.

Psalm 141: 1-2 shows us that Psalmist cries out to the Lord... *"O Lord, I call to You; come quick to me, Hear my voice when I call to You. May my prayer be set before you like incense; may the lifting up of my hands be like the evening sacrifice."*

Then, when we think -- "God did you really hear my prayers?".... some of the most calming words are spoken back to us by our Savior, *"Come to Me, all you who are weary and burdened, and I will give you rest. Take My yoke upon you and learn from Me, for I am gentle and humble in heart, and you will find rest for your souls."* (Matthew 11:28-29) Jesus is there today, ready to give you rest as you pour out your prayers.

Today, know that your prayers are like incense to the Lord. They fill the Heavens as you cry out to Him. He loves to hear you, so keep on praying, keep on seeking, keep on believing, keep on burning the midnight oil when times are difficult, because Jesus promises us that He will give us rest.

****

ASK YOURSELF:

What is God revealing to me today?

_____
_____
_____
_____
_____
_____
_____
_____

How do I see God working in my life today?

_____
_____
_____
_____
_____
_____
_____
_____

What can I do to bring a blessing to someone else?

_____
_____
_____
_____
_____
_____
_____
_____

Journey Day 28 _____

One time I was sitting in a hotel room, in the mountains of New Mexico, and was in awe of the splendor and beauty all around me. The next day my husband and I were driving through White Sands and gazing at the mountain ranges on both sides, and a song came on from the group Mercy Me. It was a song that I heard many times before... "Word of God Speak". The song is really simple, asking God to let my words be few before Him, and that I would have ears to hear Him clearly, and that He would speak through His amazing Word.

As I listened to the words of this song, I could see God speaking through the mountains all around us. The majesty of the amazing mountains that seemed to explode out of the ground, and cause the skyline to have the handwriting of God so vivid and clear. Who else could create such an incredible vision? Who else knew exactly where to place each mountain range? Who else could catch the attention of mankind by the splendor of the mountain? It was very clear that God was showing Himself and His Word through the silence of the mountains and the movement of the winds.

Simply put, the first verse of God's word was vivid... *"In the beginning God created the heavens and the earth."* Genesis 1:1. I saw this scripture in real life. Sometimes I forget that I need to put away the noise of everyday life and remember what God did for us so long ago. Take a moment to "listen to God" and let what is around you speak clearly to you.

Today, be still and silent for a moment, and let God speak clearly to you through His creation.

****

ASK YOURSELF:

What is God revealing to me today?

_____
_____
_____
_____
_____
_____
_____
_____

How do I see God working in my life today?

_____
_____
_____
_____
_____
_____
_____
_____
_____

What can I do to bring a blessing to someone else?

_____
_____
_____
_____
_____
_____
_____
_____

Journey Day 29 _____

At one time I worked in a finance department of a large company..
The specific department was Inventory. Each month I had to
reconcile some different ledger accounts. The G/L accounts must
equal all expenses that were charged against them. It really seemed
pretty easy to me... most of the time. One month was a different
story. There was an error. My numbers were not balancing. I began
looking for the error in the files that were downloaded from our
computer system. Nope, not there. Then I looked in my Excel
formula's, thinking I had an error there. Nope, not there either. So I
decided to start over and see if it was a "human error" that I had just
missed. Still, no luck in finding the error. I highlighted columns,
ran calculation's, sorted my file by dollar amounts... nothing was
showing up. As much as I hate to admit it, I spent over half a day
searching for this error. (Yes, I am telling on myself.)

As frustration started to set in, I heard this still small voice say...
"ask _**Me**_ where the error is, and I will show you." Yep, you guessed
it, I listened, I asked, and within five minutes I found the error. It
was such a simple error, right in front of my face. I thought to
myself, "how could I have missed something so easy"? How simple
it really was to find the mistake, yet I am the one that made it
difficult.

Then I realized that many times I am this way with our Lord, Jesus.
There are times when I feel like I have looked, and searched, and
done everything in my power to get God's attention, only to realize
that He is just a breath away. In Matthew 7:7 Jesus says it perfectly
– *"Ask, and it will be given to you, seek, and you will find; Knock
and the door will be opened to you. For everyone who asks - will
receive, and whoever seeks - will find, and to him who knocks - the
door will be opened."* How simple it is when we search for our
Lord. He is willing to open the door to you. Willing to give to you a
new life, a new year, a new month, a new day, a new moment, all we
have to do is ask.

Today, you may be in a struggling place. The struggle may seem
like there is no clear answer in front of you, but God knows your
heart. He will step in and open the door for you. Continue to search

my beloved, for the Lord's mighty hand and His loving heart, and surely He will meet you.

****

ASK YOURSELF:

What is God revealing to me today?

_____

_____

_____

_____

_____

_____

_____

How do I see God working in my life today?

_____

_____

_____

_____

_____

_____

_____

What can I do to bring a blessing to someone else?

_____

_____

_____

_____

_____

_____

_____

Journey Day 30 _____

I was wondering, how many of you like to go mountain climbing, or maybe rock climbing? My daughter Katy really enjoys rock climbing. She has gone with some of her friends who range in the age of 18 to 25 and they are all different shapes and sizes. Katy told me how much she really enjoyed rock climbing, even with the bruises, cuts, pains and soreness that comes along. If you have never done it, she would suggest that you climb a "rock" or take a hike in the mountain at least once. She said one of the things that was so great about rock climbing was reaching the top of the hill or mountain. Then when you get to the top of where you are climbing, it seems there is a level place to stand on. You can see how far you have climbed AND see that your friends reached the same destination as you.

Have you ever thought about the hill that Jesus had to climb up? But better yet, what about all of the different people that climbed that hill with Him? There were the centurions, the townspeople, men, women and children. There were also the High Priests and the two thieves on the crosses, and don't forget about the Scribes and the Elders of the church. Plus there was Mary, Jesus' mother, Mary the mother of James and the forgiven harlot Mary Magdalene… and of course the one man named in all four Gospels, Simon the man who carried the cross for Christ when Jesus couldn't carry it any further. **ALL** of these people "climbed the hill" but when they ALL reached the same place, it was flat and even. Everyone was equal and on level ground, with the exception of One… that was Jesus-He was above everyone, hanging on the cross.

You see, no matter who you are, where you have been, or what "status" in life you have managed to obtain or not obtain, the ground at the foot of the cross is level. We all stand in the same place before a Savior who wants to give us HIS best, HIS life, HIS grace and mercy.

To write out the story of Jesus and "the others" walking up the hill would take away from the opportunity for you to read the story yourself. I urge you to take a moment and read the last two or three chapters of Matthew or Mark or Luke or John and see the many faces of people who stood at the feet of Christ on the level ground. You are no different than any one of them. Are you the High Priest or the forgiven thief or maybe even the scorned woman who longs for forgiveness? Remember, Christ is there for you, on level ground, waiting to wrap His arms around you.

Today my prayer is that HIS blessings be poured upon each of you reading this, knowing that you are not standing on solid ground alone.

****

ASK YOURSELF:

What is God revealing to me today?

_____
_____
_____
_____
_____

How do I see God working in my life today?

_____
_____
_____
_____
_____

What can I do to bring a blessing to someone else?

_____
_____
_____
_____
_____
_____

Journey Day 31 _____

"I would sooner live in a cottage and wonder at everything, than live in a castle and wonder at nothing." - Quote by: Joan Winmill Brown

What type of house do you live in? Is it a huge house with several bedrooms, or is it a small apartment with just enough space to put everything you have in it? Or possibly a simple three bedroom, brick house in a quiet neighborhood, or maybe even in a hut in Africa. Some people are living in tents and card board boxes. Personally I live in a double-wide mobile home. Many people call them "trailers", others call it a "modular house". What I call it is "home". I read the quote above by Joan Brown and immediately thought this is exactly where I want to be. I don't want to miss out on the wonders of life.

The ultimate home that I want to live in is God's home. But, on the way I don't want to miss out on anything that HE puts before me. Sometimes the "things" that we live for, or work for get in the way of God's wonders. I know there are so many obstacles that can stop us along the way, but the "wonders" that are in front of us are just as many. One day while I was outside grilling burgers, I looked over and sitting on top of my crepe' myrtle was a baby bird. He appeared to be a "youngster". Probably just pushed out of the tree because he looked so terrified. For half an hour or so I watched this little fellow and he didn't move. What made that little baby bird sit in the tree right next to my patio? Why didn't the baby fly away? I believe it was one of God's wonders staring me right in the face. It was so small I almost missed it, but HE opened my eyes to see a marvelous sight.

What are you living for? Are you living for God's ultimate home, looking for His wonders along the way? Or, are you living day to day, in dread and suffocation of this world's stuff? Jesus gives comfort to the disciples in John 14: 1-4 - *"Do not let your hearts be troubled. Trust in God; trust also in Me. In My Father's house are many rooms; if it were not so, I would have told you. And if I go and prepare a place for you, I will come back and take you to be with Me that you also may be where I am. You know the way to the place I am going."* Isn't that wonderful, our Savior instructs us not to be troubled, because one day we will live in God's Mansion.

Today, remember to search for the wonders of life along the way.

****

ASK YOURSELF:

What is God revealing to me today?

_____
_____
_____
_____
_____
_____
_____

How do I see God working in my life today?

_____
_____
_____
_____
_____
_____

What can I do to bring a blessing to someone else?

_____
_____
_____
_____
_____

Journey Day 32 _____

Have you ever had a cracked windshield? I mean to the point that it is so cracked you have to move your head around between the cracks to see where you are going? My daughter's car windshield had many cracks. The cracks were going diagonal, horizontal, at an angle, and curving every direction you could imagine. When she bought the car it had only one tiny little crack on bottom right hand side. It wasn't even noticeable. Then a rock hit the windshield and the little crack became a huge spider vein and grew and grew until looking out the front window was almost not visible. The window was replaced and wow, it was so clear. No spider veins, no cracks, nothing to peer around to try and figure out where you were driving. I didn't realize how bad the cracks were, until the new window was put in. I could see the road so clearly now.

At times we are the same way with our walk with Christ. We start out looking through a "clean window". It is easy to see where we are going, and easy to follow Christ in the direction that He is taking us. Then a little bump comes along that causes a crack in our window. The bump could be something from our past that comes back to haunt us, or a recent problem that has taken control of us. We become so involved in the problem, that the crack begins to grow. It grows to the point that the things around us become obstacles. Even our faith may become an obstacle. We try to steer ourselves down the road of life, but more "cracks" keep appearing. We wonder, whatever happened to that "clear window"? Then all of a sudden it becomes clear... we realize that we have walked away from the window that was so full of clarity. That window is Jesus. One of my favorite passages is when the Lord is talking to Moses and to Joshua. He tells them, *"I will be with you. I will never leave your or forsake you."*

When we need the clear window, when life seems full of "spider veins"... there He is, just waiting to be put in place.

Is it time to "replace" the cracked window with the original clean window and start over? Whatever your window looks like, no matter what the problem is, He is waiting to give you clarity. Call on Him today to come and give you a new view of the road that lies ahead of you.

Today is a new day, to look out the front window with clarity.

****

ASK YOURSELF:

What is God revealing to me today?

_____
_____
_____
_____
_____
_____
_____

How do I see God working in my life today?

_____
_____
_____
_____
_____
_____

What can I do to bring a blessing to someone else?

_____
_____
_____
_____
_____

Journey Day 33 _____

I was remembering when my husband and I took a trip down to Lake Houston to stay with some friends in their lake house for the weekend. It was going to be a nice relaxing weekend with no headaches, hassels or costs. Our goal was to just sit on the porch looking out over the beautiful lake. Well, you know the old saying "best laid plans go astray"…

Friday night on the way down to the city, our car began to have a problem. Bill pulled into a gas station and smoke was billowing out from the engine. We sat parked at the station for about 30 minutes, waiting for the smoke to go away so that we could see the real issue. Bill poured coolant and water into the radiator and as quickly as he poured it in, it poured out the back part of the engine and trickled down the parking lot. We were right next door to a hotel and we managed to get the car parked in the hotel parking lot. We knew we had to do something the next morning. We decided to make a trek, by foot, back to the gas station to find out if there were any local mechanics on duty in this small town.

Now the "trek" was through a soggy, stickery, tall weeds and grass, field. We headed out and began walking in two separate paths but going in the same direction. Immediately I stepped in a HUGE hole, then a mud puddle, and plenty of stickers were sticking me. So, I looked at Bill, there he was just walking with no problems. So, I decided to get back over to where he was and I followed right behind him. I stepped exactly where he stepped. He was going before me and I knew what the safe place was to step in. I don't even know if Bill knew what I was doing. But, we made it safely to the road that led to the gas station.

While I was walking behind Bill, God reminded me of the scripture in John… 8:12, *"then Jesus spoke to them again, saying, 'I Am the light of the world. He who follows Me shall not walk in darkness, but have the light of life.'"* No matter where you are standing, as long as we stand in the footsteps of Jesus there will be light. No matter where you are walking, if you walk in the path of Jesus Christ, you will have light. You may feel like you are standing in a deep fog, or a walking in mud holes, but Jesus has made this promise that we WILL have the light of life and NOT walk in darkness.

Today if you feel you are walking in darkness or in mud holes, know that you are not alone, Jesus is beside you.

****

ASK YOURSELF:

What is God revealing to me today?

_____
_____
_____
_____
_____
_____
_____

How do I see God working in my life today?

_____
_____
_____
_____
_____
_____
_____

What can I do to bring a blessing to someone else?

_____
_____
_____
_____
_____
_____
_____

Journey Day 34 _____

North Texas was receiving its fair share of rain and thunderstorms. Once when I was out of town, my husband called me and told me that he did not sleep well due to the storms. I thought for a few seconds why he didn't sleep well, then he continued to tell me that it wasn't the actual storm, but it was our 20 pound kitty, Samson that kept him awake through the night. Samson really doesn't like storms, and I must admit that I have spoiled him a little when it does storm. At the first sound of thunder or lightening, Samson is on the bed, making his way to my king size pillow to lay right next to my head. My thinking is the closer he is, the more protected he feels. The problem was that my husband was laying in my spot, so Samson took it upon himself to do what he normally does when he is afraid... lay right next to Bill's head. If Bill moved, Samson moved. If Bill rolled over, Samson scooted closer. Bill said that Samson was really afraid and shaking, but he was also annoying. Samson knew where to go when he was afraid. Samson also knew that Bill, or myself, would comfort him to the best of our "cat"ability and pet him and let him know that everything would be okay. Of course the storm lasted most of the night, so Bill didn't get much sleep, but Samson slept like a baby. He felt safe and protected.

How many times in my own life have I felt afraid of a situation that I was in, or frightened of? Like the storm that rolled in at our house, and the storms that roll into our lives, we do have a "safe place" to go. One of my favorite promises from God is in Isaiah 40:11 - He tells us, *"Fear not for I am with you. Be not dismayed for I am your God and I will strengthen you. Yes, I will help you, I will uphold you with MY righteous right hand."*

Wow, does God really and truly give us strength? Does He really help in our times of need? Will He take the fear away? These are really tough questions when you are standing in the storm. Samson knew that he would be taken care of if he just went to the right place... to the king size pillow laying next to Bill. The fear was familiar to Samson, but he remembered where to run to, in his time of fear.

Today, if you are in a place that you feel fear is standing right next to you, run to the familiar place of the "King's throne" and lay next to Him. He is there ready to hold you close and keep you safe in His righteous right hand.

****

ASK YOURSELF:

What is God revealing to me today?

_____

_____

_____

_____

_____

_____

_____

How do I see God working in my life today?

_____

_____

_____

_____

_____

_____

_____

What can I do to bring a blessing to someone else?

_____

_____

_____

_____

_____

_____

_____

Journey Day 35 _____

Have you ever lost anything? Have you ever been on a trip
somewhere and left something behind? Or you planned a trip to be
somewhere and you got where you were going and realized you left
something at home that you desperately needed? I imagine the
answer would be yes from most of us. I have done all three of
these. Once I was staying in a hotel and I had taken my jewelry off
and laid it on the bathroom counter. My jewelry consisted of a pair
of silver hoop earrings, a pearl ring that my daughter gave me, a
Sylvester watch (yes, that is Sylvester the cat) and a ring that I
inherited when my mother passed away. The next day came and we
left to go to our next destination.

We hadn't been there more than five minutes and my heart sank….
You guessed it, I left my jewelry sitting on the bathroom counter at
the hotel. I wasn't too concerned about the watch and earrings, but
both of the rings meant more to me than just being a ring. They
were "heirlooms" to me. How could I have done such a ridiculous
thing? What was I thinking? Didn't these "things" mean more to
me than just jewelry? Of course they did but that doesn't mean I left
them there on purpose. As a matter of fact, I was so excited to be
able to see an old friend that day, I just wanted to get where we were
going, and didn't even think about the jewelry. But when I realized
what I had done, my heart sank. I ran to where Bill was and told him
what I had done. He immediately called the hotel and he said he
would drive back and pick up my jewelry. I waited for Bill to come
back and I prayed. I asked God to please watch over these special
things and to remember how "invaluable" and important they were
to me. A little while later Bill walks in with the jewelry. I thanked
him and thanked God for taking care of me in my time of
"senselessness".

Immediately God was showing me that we do the same thing with
Him. We will be going along and know that God, the Holy Spirit
and Jesus Christ are with us everywhere we are. Life then gets
REALLY busy, and very filled up and we keep going on the paths
that seem so crazy and chaotic that we just leave Jesus behind. Then
we begin to feel that feeling of "oh no, I've lost Him… how do I get
Him back, where can I go look for Him?" Unlike the jewelry in the

hotel, I don't think I remember the places that I have left Jesus behind. Also, unlike the jewelry in the hotel, when I do leave Him behind, he will not stay there. The jewelry couldn't follow me, but God gives us a promise in Deuteronomy 31:6 and Joshua 1:5... "I will never leave you or forsake you." Isn't that too grand! We can walk away from God, (or try to), but HE will not walk away from us, OR stay sitting on the counter. I tell you today, if you have felt like there is no way for you to reach out to Jesus, or that you have gone on a trip so far away that He couldn't find you, it is absolutely not true. Stretch out your hand to the sky and let Him touch you today.

Today, God is standing there right next to you... just slip Him on your finger, and feel His touch in your heart. He is the "heirloom" of your life, and He wants to be worn in your heart.

****

ASK YOURSELF:

What is God revealing to me today?

_____
_____
_____
_____

How do I see God working in my life today?

_____
_____
_____
_____

What can I do to bring a blessing to someone else?

_____
_____
_____
_____
_____

After reading these life stories, I have one question left – do you know Jesus?

The Word tells us that all have sinned and fall short of the glory of God, and are justified freely by His grace through the redemption that came by Christ Jesus. God sacrificed Jesus on the altar of the world to clear the world of sin. Having faith in Him sets us in the clear. God decided on this course of action in full view of the public – to set the world in the clear with Himself through the sacrifice of Jesus, finally taking care of the sins He had so patiently endured. This is not only clear, but it's now – this is current history! God sets things right. He also makes it possible for us to live in His rightness.

If you have never asked Jesus to come into your heart, pray this simple prayer:

"Jesus, forgive me, for I am a sinner. Come into my heart and lead me each day of my life. Thank You Jesus for loving me so much that you would sacrifice Your life for me. I am Yours and You are mine today and through all eternity. Amen."

If you prayed this prayer, tell someone. Or send an email to **sandy@prodigalpublishing.today,** and we will celebrate with you.

All praises to our King!

> *"But encourage one another daily, as long as it called <u>Today,</u> so that none of you may be hardened by sin's deceitfulness."*- Hebrews 3:13.

For more information about the Journey Series Books, or volume discounts, please email **sandy@prodigalpublishing.today.** You can also purchase this book on Amazon.com or through Kindle.

Thank you for your prayers and support!

Joyfully in Him!

Made in the USA
Columbia, SC
25 August 2022

65920100R00052